W9-AUY-707

Rookie STAR™ Fact Finder

10 Fascinating Facts About Castles

14R4B

By Jessica Cohn

Content Consultant
Professor Sarah Peverley
University of Liverpool

Reading Consultant
Jeanne M. Clidas, Ph.D.
Reading Specialist

Children's Press®
An Imprint of Scholastic Inc.

Boyle County Public Library

Table of Contents

Introduction

The Middle Ages was the time from the years 476 to 1500. In those days, most land belonged to kings and queens. They had to fight to keep their power and territory. Rulers had to build strong castles to keep out their enemies.

Do you want to learn more fascinating facts about castles? Then read on!

FACT 1

Walls were filled with junk

Walls were wide so guards could walk along the top.

Some castle walls were up to 20 feet wide. That is more than twice as wide as a school bus.

Builders used large stones for the sides. They filled the inside with broken building materials. Then they sealed up the walls.

It could take up to 20 years to build a castle. Straw and dung were used to protect unfinished walls from winter weather.

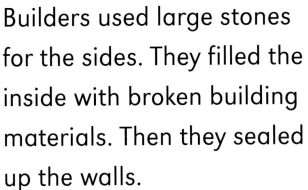

Over 12,000 castles were built in Europe

European kings gave away different parts of their land to lords. The lords had

This is what is left of Rabi Castle in the Czech Republic.

castles built on their property. They protected that part of the king's land.

A lot of lords became rich by serving as knights. Knights were the king's top warriors. They were trained to fight on horseback.

FACT 3

Lords often brought beds when visiting

In the early Middle Ages, many castles did not have a lot of furniture. They did not even have bedrooms. People just slept in one part of the great hall of the castle. For this reason, when lords

This is a lord's bed from the Middle Ages.

visited other castles, they usually brought their beds with them. They often brought their own bathtubs, too! Sleeping chambers became more popular as time went on.

Often, the most important thing inside the castle walls was a well. When the castle was under **siege**, people needed water to survive.

FACT 4

Castles did not have bathrooms

The toilets were called **garderobes**. They were really just holes in the floor. The mess ran

This hard stone bench is a garderobe.

down the outside walls. The person in charge of clearing away the mess was called a gong farmer.

The garderobe is behind this wall.

You would not want to be standing under this spot at the wrong time!

Attackers sometimes came in through garderobes! This happened in 1204 during a battle between England and France. *Yuck!* Some people added bars to the hole to keep enemies out.

FACT 5

Castles were dirty, inside and out

Inside the castle, the floors were covered with dried straw. Food and animal poop often ended up on the floor. Even when the straw was changed, bits of food, bones, and poop were left behind. Castle workers put dried flowers down to cover the stink.

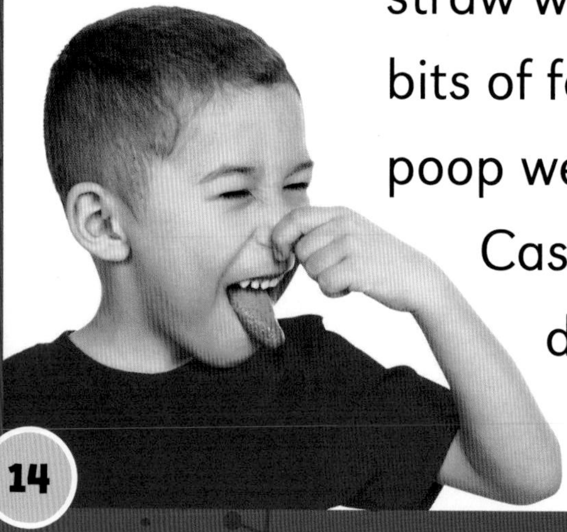

There were no air fresheners in the Middle Ages.

Dogs and cats roamed in the buildings and pathways. The animals had a job, too—chasing rats!

FACT 6

Rich people ate off big pieces of stale bread

In those days, lords and ladies used bread as plates. These plates were called trenchers.

Servants prepare for a feast. On special occasions, hundreds of people would eat at the castle.

People ate greasy food, such as boars, deer, and rabbits. When their trencher got soggy, they ate it or gave it to beggars.

Fresh food rotted fast in the days before refrigerators. A lot of people ate meat that was dried out with lots of salt.

Only some lords and ladies had knives and spoons. Forks were not in use yet.

FACT 7

A castle was like a giant rattrap

Castles were built with special defenses.

The walls had **merlons** on the top. Soldiers could fire at attackers through

the gaps and then hide behind the merlons. They could also shoot arrows out through slit-like windows.

Ceilings had holes so people could drop burning objects and hot oil on attackers below. The cutouts were called murder holes.

FACT 8

Castles had crazy defenses

Enemies used a siege tower to reach the top of a castle's walls.

When a castle was under attack, people inside raised the drawbridge.

This made it hard for attackers to cross the moat. It also sealed off the castle entrance. During the battle, both sides threw fire at each other. People in the castle even threw sick people and diseased animals at attackers!

It is harder for animal hides to catch fire than wood. So large wooden weapons, such as **siege towers**, were often covered with animal hides.

9 The best weapon might have been a pick

This knight is trying to undermine the castle wall.

Attackers used picks to dig tunnels under castle walls. This was called undermining. The attackers

often set fires in those tunnels. When the ground caved in, the walls fell down. That helped the attackers get inside.

Many castles had dry moats around them. These big ditches helped stop siege machines and undermining.

A moat was a deep, wide ditch surrounding the whole castle.

FACT 10

Prague Castle is as big as seven football fields

It is the biggest castle in the world. Prague Castle was built about 1200 years ago. Attackers burned it several times over the

Visitors gather at the entrance to the castle at Prague.

centuries. Each time, it was fixed. Now it covers 18 acres.

The biggest castle that people still live in is Windsor Castle. It is in Great Britain. It covers 13 acres. Windsor Castle is one of the homes of the ruler of England.

Boyle County Public Library

Activity

Make a Castle of Your Own

Follow the instructions to make your own castle from recyclables.

You Will Need:

- ✔ scissors
- ✔ cardboard box
- ✔ pencil
- ✔ string
- ✔ glue
- ✔ four empty paper towel tubes
- ✔ flat piece of cardboard for the base
- ✔ crayons, paints, or colored pencils

1 To learn more about castle architecture, do research! Ask a grown-up to help you search the Internet. Use this book and others from the library.

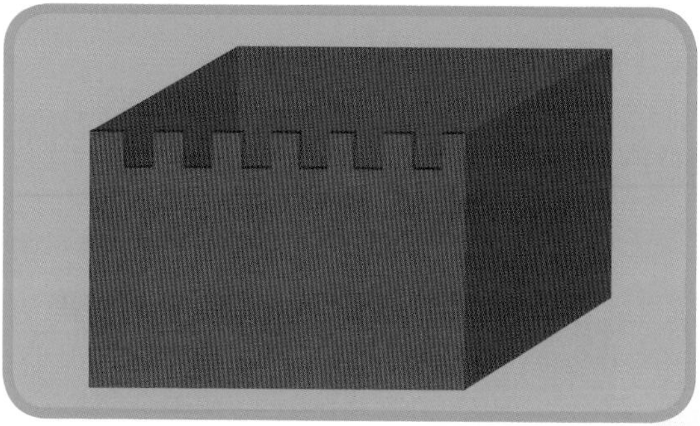

2 Cut the top flaps off the box. To make merlons along the top of the box, draw a series of squares all around the top edge. Then cut out every other square to leave merlons sticking up.

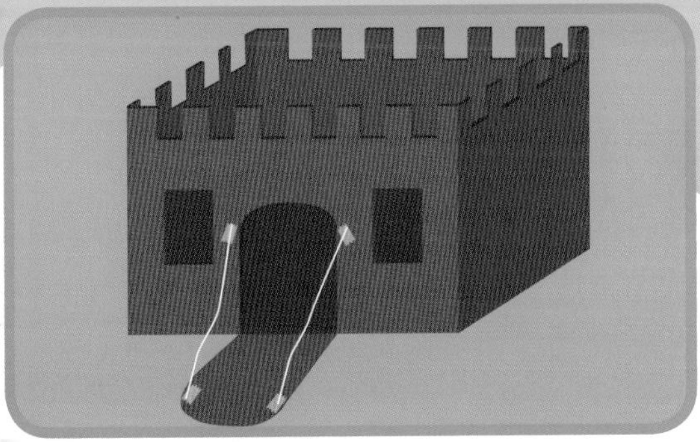

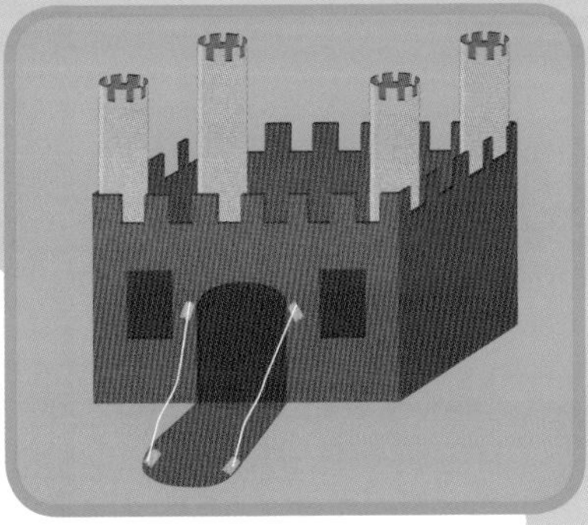

3 Draw an arch on the front of the box, right in the center. Cut out the arch, but leave the bottom attached. This will be your drawbridge. Attach some string to the drawbridge, and thread it through small holes in the front of the castle. Draw windows next to the drawbridge and cut them out.

4 Cut merlons on the paper towel tubes. Glue one into each corner of the castle.

5 Place the castle on the cardboard base and decorate. Color the castle gray and draw in "stones." Add a moat to the cardboard base, as well as some grass.

Timeline

In the Middle Ages, people ate together in the castle's great hall.

The Middle Ages begin in Europe.

5th century | **9th century** | **10th century** | **13th century**

9th century: Early castles in Europe are made of dirt and timber.

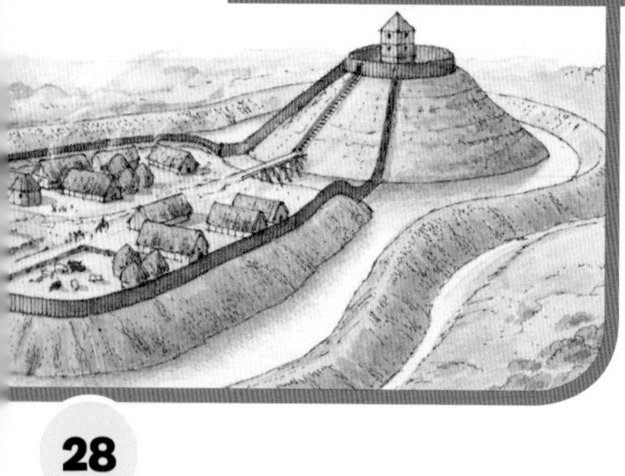

10th century: Rich lords start building castles with stone.

13th century: Castles are built with more than one wall around them.

Gunpowder and guns come into use across Europe.

The Middle Ages end in Europe. Now, cannons are powerful enough to break stone walls.

14th century | **15th century** | **16th century** | **2017**

Forts are built as needed, but the great age of castles ends.

Britain's Windsor Castle is the biggest castle that is still lived in.

Glossary

- **garderobes** (GAR-deh-rohbs): lavatories in the Middle Ages

- **merlons** (MUR-lins): upright parts at the top of walls built with ridges

- **siege** (SEEJ): army operation in which fighters surround and cut off a town or fort

- **siege towers** (SEEJ TOU-ers): ladders or steps covered by a tower and put on wheels

Index

About the Author

As a girl, Jessica Cohn used to play in the spiral staircase at the Detroit Institute of Arts, in Michigan, pretending it was the Middle Ages. Now she lives in California with her family. She enjoys hiking, helping student writers, and writing books like this one. She also likes exploring. Hey, there are castles all over the world!

Facts for Now

Visit this Scholastic Web site for more information on castles:

www.factsfornow.scholastic.com

Enter the keyword **Castles**

Library of Congress Cataloging-in-Publication Data
Names: Cohn, Jessica, author.
Title: 10 fascinating facts about castles/by Jessica Cohn.
Other titles: Ten fascinating facts about castles
Description: New York : Children's Press, 2017. | Series: Rookie star. Fact finder | Includes index.
Identifiers: LCCN 2016030337 | ISBN 9780531222591 (library binding) | ISBN 9780531226759 (pbk.)
Subjects: LCSH: Castles—Europe—Juvenile literature.
Classification: LCC NA7710 .C56 2017 | DDC 728.8/1—dc23
LC record available at https://lccn.loc.gov/2016030337

No part of this publication may be reproduced in whole or in part, or stored in a retrieval system, or transmitted in any form or by any means, electronic, mechanical, photocopying, recording, or otherwise, without written permission of the publisher. For information regarding permission, write to Scholastic Inc., Attention: Permissions Department, 557 Broadway, New York, NY 10012.

Produced by Spooky Cheetah Press
Design by Judith Christ-Lafond

© 2017 by Scholastic Inc.

All rights reserved. Published in 2017 by Children's Press, an imprint of Scholastic Inc.

Printed in China 62

SCHOLASTIC, CHILDREN'S PRESS, ROOKIE STAR™ FACT FINDER, and associated logos are trademarks and/or registered trademarks of Scholastic Inc.

1 2 3 4 5 6 7 8 9 10 R 26 25 24 23 22 21 20 19 18 17

Photographs ©: cover castle: Spaces Images/Getty Images; cover background, back cover background: stock09/Shutterstock, Inc.; back cover cannon: Alain Machet (3)/Alamy Images; 2 top: DEA/G. Dagli Orti/Getty Images; 2 bottom, 3 bottom left: Henk Meijer/Alamy Images; 3 bottom right: North Wind Picture Archives; 4 arch: Image Wizard/Shutterstock, Inc.; 4-5 background: blickwinkel/Alamy Images; 5 girl: Thomas M Perkins/Shutterstock, Inc.; 6-7 main: Andrey Lebedev/Shutterstock, Inc.; 7 top: Eag1eEyes/Shutterstock, Inc.; 8-9 main: Kletr/Shutterstock, Inc.; 9 top: Nejron Photo/Fotolia; 10: Renata Sedmakova/Shutterstock, Inc.; 11: Print Collector/Getty Images; 12 bottom left: Wolfgang Kaehler/LightRocket/Getty Images; 12 bottom right: bokan/Fotolia; 13 bottom: CSP_alessandro0770/age fotostock; 13 top: Sergei Kazakov/Dreamstime; 14: 3445128471Shutterstock, Inc.; 15: DEA/G. Dagli Orti/Getty Images; 16: ullstein bild/The Granger Collection; 17 bottom: artkamalov/Shutterstock, Inc.; 17 top bread: kak2s/Shutterstock, Inc.; 17 top meat: Jiri Hera/Shutterstock, Inc.; 18: Hulton Archive/Getty Images; 19 left: Jose Ignacio Soto/Shutterstock, Inc.; 19 right: Heritage Images/Getty Images; 20-21 main: Dorling Kindersley/Getty Images; 21 top right background: Chiyacat/Shutterstock, Inc.; 21 top right torch: Nejron Photo/Fotolia; 22: Duncan Walker/Getty Images; 23: StockPhotosArt/Shutterstock, Inc.; 24: Paul Springett B/Alamy Images; 25 top: robertharding/Alamy Images; 25 bottom: Paul Springett B/Alamy Images; 26-27 illustrations: Keith Plechaty; 26-27 craft girl: Valua Vitaly/Shutterstock, Inc.; 28 bottom: Dorling Kindersley/Getty Images; 28 top: ullstein bild/The Granger Collection; 29 top left: NYPL/Science Source/Getty Images; 29 bottom: robertharding/Alamy Images; 29 top right: Alain Machet (3)/Alamy Images; 30 top: Wolfgang Kaehler/LightRocket/Getty Images; 30 center top: Jose Ignacio Soto/Shutterstock, Inc.; 30 center bottom: Print Collector/Getty Images; 30 bottom: North Wind Picture Archives.

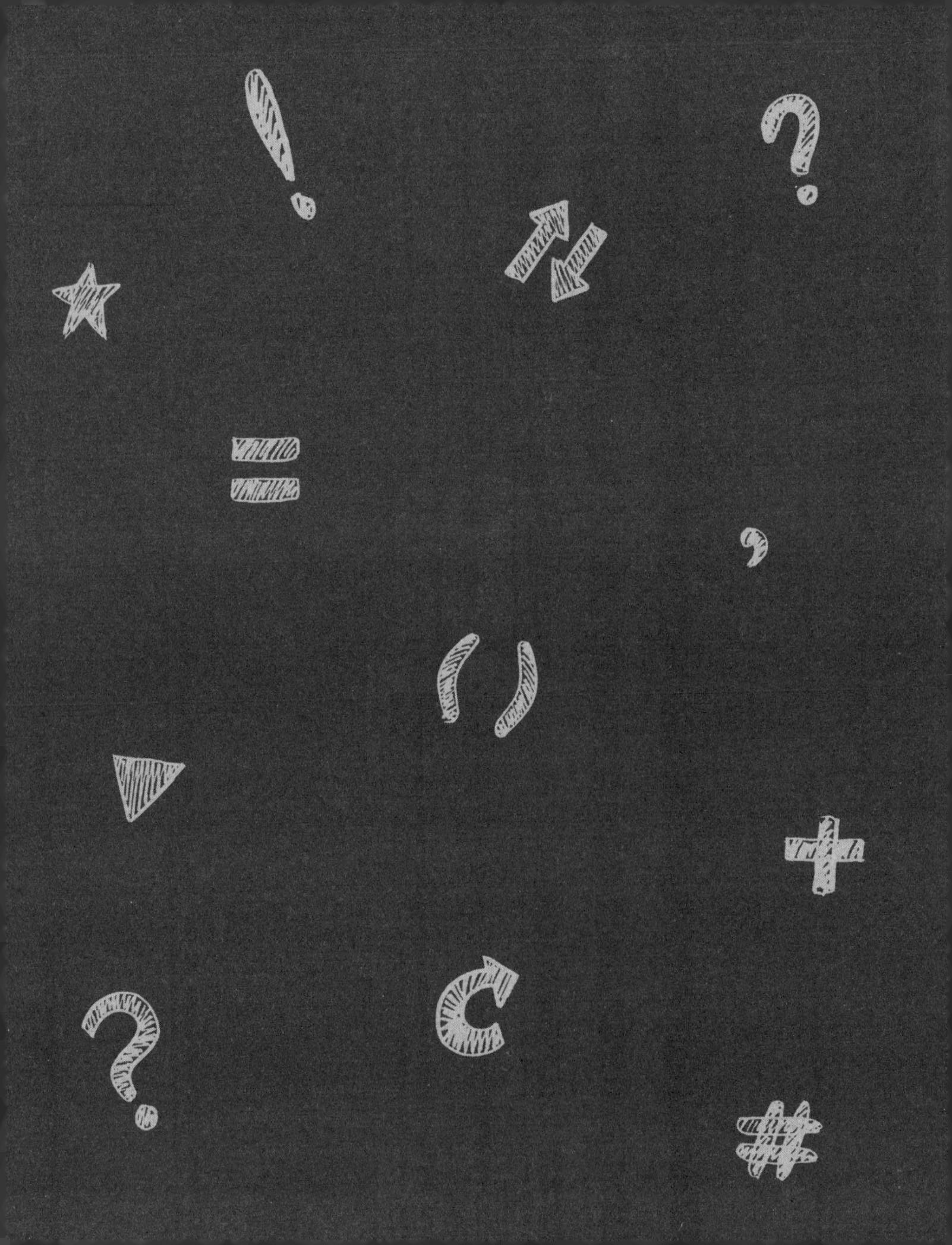